DRAW WITH GRANDMA

THE TWO-PERSON DOODLE BOOK

Please write a review on amazon.

YOUR KIND REVIEWS AND HONEST COMMENTS GO ALONG
WAY IN HELPING US CREATE MORE BOOKS LIKE THIS.

Thank you!

1

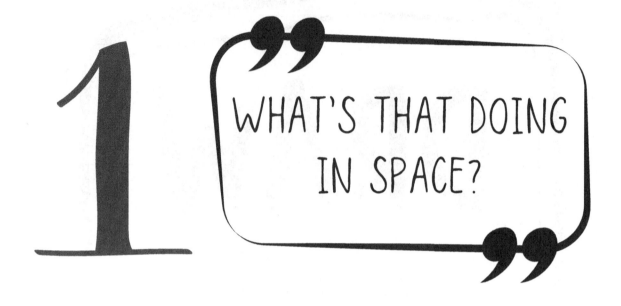

> WHAT'S THAT DOING IN SPACE?

CHILD

IMAGINE OUTER SPACE. DRAW THE EARTH, THE SUN, AND SOME BRIGHT STARS.

GRANDMA

DRAW SOMETHING STRANGE FLOATING IN SPACE.

2 "THE MONKEY'S BIRTHDAY"

CHILD

DRAW A MONKEY
WEARING A
BIRTHDAY HAT.

GRANDMA

DRAW ALL THE
BIRTHDAY
DECORATIONS AND
DON'T FORGET THE
CAKE!

3

CHILD

DRAW THE SKY
WITH THE BIGGEST
RAINBOW YOU CAN
IMAGINE.

GRANDMA

DRAW AN UNUSUAL
TREASURE AT THE
END OF THE
RAINBOW.

4

THE SINGING RAINBOOTS

CHILD

DRAW YOUR
FAVORITE RAINBOOTS.

GRANDMA

DRAW A SILLY FACE
ON THE RAIN BOOTS
THAT MAKES THEM
LOOK LIKE THEY'RE
SINGING.

5

CHILD

DRAW YOUR FAVORITE
SHAPE AND TURN IT
INTO A SILLY FACE.

GRANDMA

DRAW YOUR FAVORITE
SHAPE AND TURN IT
INTO A SILLY FACE.

6

THE MELTING SNOWMAN

CHILD

DRAW A SNOWMAN THATS STARTING TO MELT.

GRANDMA

DRAW THE SCENERY. A BIG PALM TREE, SAND AND ANYTHING ELSE YOU FIND ON THE BEACH.

7

THE DUAL-COLORED HOUSE

CHILD

DRAW ONE SIDE OF A HOUSE IN ONE COLOR.

GRANDMA

DRAW THE OTHER SIDE OF THE HOUSE IN A DIFFERENT COLOR.

8

THE SILLY ALIEN

CHILD

DRAW AN ALIEN
WEARING A SILLY
OUTFIT.

GRANDMA

DRAW THE PLANET
THAT THE SILLY
ALIEN IS FROM.

CHILD

DRAW THE COOLEST TREE HOUSE YOU CAN IMAGINE.

GRANDMA

DRAW OCEAN SCENERY AND FISH SURROUNDING THE TREE HOUSE.

CHILD

DRAW A BIG CAMPFIRE, A TENT, AND OTHER CAMPING SUPPLIES.

GRANDMA

DRAW A SQUIRREL ROASTING A MARSHMALLOW OVER THE FIRE.

11

MY SUPERHERO!

CHILD

DRAW YOURSELF AS SUPERHERO! WHAT SUPER POWERS WOULD YOU HAVE?

GRANDMA

DRAW AN ANIMAL THAT NEEDS TO BE RESCUED BY YOUR SUPERHERO.

12

THE COOL BUTTERFLY

CHILD

DRAW A BEAUTIFUL
BUTTERFLY
WEARING
SUNGLASSES.

GRANDMA

DRAW A GARDEN
FULL OF FLOWERS
FOR THE BUTTERFLY.

13

"DOUGHNUTS IN SPACE?"

CHILD

DRAW AN ASTRONAUT FLOATING IN OUTER SPACE.

GRANDMA

DRAW SOME OF YOUR FAVORITE DOUGHNUTS FLOATING AROUND THE ASTRONAUT.

14

CHRISTMAS TIME

CHILD

DRAW A BIG CHRISTMAS TREE WITH ALL YOUR FAVOURITE ORNAMENTS.

GRANDMA

DRAW SANTA PUTTING PRESENTS UNDER THE CHRISTMAS TREE.

15

CHILD

DRAW A FARM WITH A BIG BARN.

GRANDMA

DRAW ANIMALS THAT DON'T BELONG ON A FARM.

16

THE JAR OF GOODIES

CHILD

DRAW A BIG GLASS JAR.

GRANDMA

DRAW SOME OF YOUR CHILD'S FAVORITE TREATS INSIDE.

17

"HOT AND COLD"

CHILD

DRAW SOMETHING
THAT IS HOT.

GRANDMA

DRAW SOMETHING
THAT IS COLD.

18

THE CASTLE

CHILD

DRAW THE BIGGEST
CASTLE THAT YOU
CAN IMAGINE.

GRANDMA

DRAW THE GUARD
DRAGON THAT
PROTECTS THE
CASTLE.

19

IT'S RAINING FOOD

CHILD

DRAW A SKY FULL OF CLOUDS.

GRANDMA

DRAW SOME OF YOUR FAVORITE FOODS FALLING FROM THE CLOUDS.

20 "THE CLEANING ROBOT"

CHILD

DRAW A SILLY
ROBOT THAT CLEANS.

GRANDMA

DRAW ALL THE
GARBAGE AND TOYS
THAT THE ROBOT
MUST CLEAN UP.

21

"SIDE BY SIDE TREES"

CHILD

DRAW A TREE WITH ITS TONGUE STICKING OUT.

GRANDMA

DRAW ANOTHER TREE WAVING AT THE FIRST TREE.

22

THE TREASURE MAP

CHILD

DRAW A BIG
TREASURE MAP
WITH LOTS OF COOL
PLACES ON IT.

GRANDMA

DRAW A TREASURE
FILLED WITH CANDY
AT THE END OF THE
MAP.

23

"MY NAME"

CHILD

DRAW ALPHABET
LETTERS WITH ARMS
AND LEGS SPELLING
YOUR NAME.

GRANDMA

DECORATE THE
LETTERS WITH A
FUN DESIGN.

24

FAMILY OF CUPCAKES

CHILD

DRAW A BABY
CUPCAKE HOLDING A
BOTTLE.

GRANDMA

DRAW THE MOM
AND DAD
CUPCAKES.

25

CHILD

DRAW A GIRAFFE WITH A VERY LONG NECK.

GRANDMA

DRAW A TUTU, NECKLACE, AND A TOP HAT ON THE GIRAFFE.

26

GO-DOG

CHILD

DRAW A BIG FISH
TANK.

GRANDMA

DRAW MINI DOGS
SWIMMING IN THE
FISH TANK.

FLOAT AWAY CARS

CHILD

DRAW A TOY CAR, A TOY TRACTOR, AND A TRUCK.

GRANDMA

DRAW BALLOONS ABOVE ALL THE VEHICLES SO THEY WILL FLOAT AWAY.

28

SPAGHETTI POOL

CHILD

DRAW A SWIMMING POOL FILLED WITH SPAGHETTI AND SAUCE.

GRANDMA

DRAW A PERSON ABOUT TO JUMP INTO THE SPAGHETTI POOL.

29

COMBINED HOLIDAY

CHILD

DRAW A FEW ITEMS
FROM YOUR
FAVORITE HOLIDAY.

GRANDMA

DRAW SOME ITEMS
FROM YOUR
FAVORITE HOLIDAY.

30

PAPER ON THE RUN

CHILD

DRAW A PAIR OF SCISSORS WITH LEGS CHASING A PIECE OF PAPER.

GRANDMA

DRAW A PIECE OF PAPER RUNNING AWAY FROM THE SCISSORS.

31

CHILD

DRAW AN AIRPLANE IN THE SKY.

GRANDMA

DRAW A CHICKEN SKYDIVING OUT OF THE AIRPLANE. DON'T FORGET THE PARACHUTE!

32

"SNOW COWBOY"

CHILD

DRAW A POLAR BEAR
IN ANTARCTICA.

GRANDMA

DRAW A COWBOY
RIDING THE POLAR
BEAR.

33

"TINY"

CHILD

WRITE THE WORD "TINY" IN HUGE BLOCK LETTERS.

GRANDMA

DRAW LITTLE BUGS LOOKING UP AT IT.

34

CHILD

DRAW ONE SOCK
WITH A COOL DESIGN
ON IT.

GRANDMA

DRAW THE OTHER
SOCK WITH A
DIFFERENT DESIGN
ON IT.

35

"I LOVE..."

CHILD

DRAW SOMETHING
YOU LOVE ABOUT
YOUR GRANDMA.

GRANDMA

DRAW SOMETHING
YOU LOVE ABOUT
YOUR GRANDCHILD.

36

"CAT CHASING A DOG"

CHILD

DRAW A CAT
CHASING AFTER A
DOG.

GRANDMA

DRAW THE DOG
RUNNING AWAY FROM
THE CAT.

37

"MR. AND MRS. MONSTER"

CHILD

DRAW A SILLY
LOOKING BOY
MONSTER.

GRANDMA

DRAW A SILLY
LOOKING GIRL
MONSTER.

38

VEGGIE GYM

CHILD

DRAW A POTATO
DOING JUMPING
JACKS.

GRANDMA

DRAW A PIECE OF
BROCCOLI LIFTING
WEIGHTS.

39

"SWEET HOT AIR BALLOON"

CHILD

DRAW A HOT AIR BALLOON IN THE SKY.

GRANDMA

DRAW SOME OF YOUR CHILDS FAVORITE CANDIES INSIDE THE HOT AIR BALLOON.

40

UPSIDE-DOWN WORLD

CHILD

DRAW PEOPLE WALKING UPSIDE DOWN AT THE TOP OF THE PAPER.

GRANDMA

DRAW THE SCENERY. UPSIDE-DOWN BUILDINGS, TREES, CARS, ETC.

41

BACKWARDS ZOO

CHILD

DRAW A ZOO EXHIBIT FOR A PERSON TO LIVE IN. MAYBE THEY HAVE A COUCH AND TV IN IT.

GRANDMA

DRAW A MONKEY WITH A CAMERA TAKING PICTURES OF THE PERSON.

42

WHO IS RIDING IT?

CHILD

DRAW A COLORFUL
BICYCLE WITH 5 SEATS
AND 7 WHEELS.

GRANDMA

DRAW DIFFERENT
DINOSAURS RIDING
THE BIKE.

43

> PIRATE SHIP FROM ANOTHER PLANET

CHILD

DRAW A PIRATE SHIP IN THE MIDDLE OF THE OCEAN.

GRANDMA

DRAW ALIENS FROM ANOTHER PLANET ON THE PIRATE SHIP.

44

THE FUNNY T-SHIRT

CHILD

DRAW A LARGE BEAR WEARING A T-SHIRT.

GRANDMA

DRAW SOMETHING FUNNY ON THE T-SHIRT.

45

THE SWINGING....

CHILD

DRAW A JUNGLE WITH VINES BETWEEN THE TREES.

GRANDMA

DRAW AN ANIMAL OTHER THAN A MONKEY SWINGING ON THE VINES.

46

THREE P'S

CHILD

DRAW RAIN CLOUDS
AND A GIANT PUDDLE.

GRANDMA

DRAW A POODLE IN
THE PUDDLE WITH A
PADDLE.

FAIRY TALE GONE WRONG

CHILD

DRAW A HANDSOME
PRINCE WITH A CROWN.

GRANDMA

DRAW A FROG
PRINCESS WITH A
CROWN.

48

SEA CREATURE WORLD

CHILD

DRAW A SET OF STAIRS GOING DOWN UNDER WATER TO A SEA CREATURE WORLD.

GRANDMA

DRAW DIFFERENT TYPES OF SEA CREATURES.

49

THE SURFING SNAIL

CHILD

DRAW THE CUTEST SNAIL YOU CAN IMAGINE.

GRANDMA

DRAW A SURFBOARD UNDER THE SNAIL AND SOME BIG WAVES.

GOING TO SPACE

CHILD

IMAGINE YOU WERE
GOING INTO SPACE.
DRAW YOURSELF IN A
ROCKET SHIP.

GRANDMA

DRAW SOME THINGS
YOU WOULD MAKE
SURE YOUR CHILD
BRINGS.

Made in the USA
Las Vegas, NV
29 November 2024